HOT RODS
and Cool Customs

Text and Photographs by
PAT GANAHL

HOT RODS
and Cool Customs

ARTABRAS
A Division of Abbeville Publishing Group
New York · London · Paris

Editor: Nancy Grubb
Designer: Celia Fuller
Production Editor: Owen Dugan
Production Manager: Lou Bilka

First edition
10 9 8 7 6 5 4 3 2

Library of Congress Cataloging-in-Publication Data
Ganahl, Pat.
   Hot rods and cool customs / text and photographs by Pat Ganahl.
        p.   cm.
   Includes index.
   ISBN 0-89660-065-3
   1. Hot rods—History. 2. Automobiles—Customizing—United States—History. I. Title.
TL236.3.G36   1996
629.228′0973—dc20   95-50262

Front cover: A 1960s-style chopped and flamed '32 three-window highboy, with big 'n' little tires on Halibrand mags and a Moon fuel tank in front of the grille.

Back cover, background: Pearl magenta flames with orange pinstripe outlines on candy red; foreground: a '56 Dodge taillight with '59 Cadillac lenses.

Frontispiece: Cool custom cruisers gathered at the drive-in, just as they did in the 1950s.

Contents

Night cruising in a full-fendered, chopped '34 five-window coupe.

Introduction

The hot rod is a uniquely American phenomenon. Where else would you expect young people to take a mass-produced, supposedly utilitarian appliance—the automobile—and strip, chop, weld, paint, and otherwise modify it into a one-off (i.e., unique), customized, often rebellious personal statement? It is inherent in American culture to want to change things, to fix things, to fiddle with things to make them suit our fancy, but hot rodding and car customizing go well beyond this. They began as a fad and quickly grew into a cult with its own styles and attitudes. Hot rodders hung out together at corner gas stations or malt shops, wore jackets emblazoned with intimidating names and icons, and spoke an arcane language about "gow jobs" and "soup ups." And even though hot rodding has changed in many ways over the decades, growing tremendously in popularity and acceptance during the last twenty years, its culture still has the same compulsions at its core: do it yourself, individualize it, make it better than—or at least different from—the mass-produced offerings, be a renegade.

Actually, all the first automobile builders at the turn of the century were hot rodders of sorts, and it was Henry Ford in particular who pioneered the stripping down and hopping up of assembly-line autos. Of course it was Ford and his Model T that begat assembly-line automobiles, but he was also the first of many to modify them. From the beginning, Ford built high-powered one-off cars and raced them to help promote his fledgling company. When he finally settled on the low-cost, lightweight, mass-marketed Model T, he delighted in using stripped and modified versions of it to pass the big, expensive Stutzes, Mercedeses, and Duesenbergs in winning major races or setting world records. That's the hot rodding spirit. Such modified Model T's even raced, and placed, in the Indianapolis 500 during the 1920s. Numerous small aftermarket companies—notably the Chevrolet brothers, with their Frontenac cylinder heads—produced thousands of hop-up parts for Model T speedsters. This activity was widespread in the Midwest, East, and South during the 1920s, but it was relegated primarily to racing on county-fair horse tracks and other dirt ovals. It was a precedent to, but not a part of, the culture that would one day be called hot rodding.

Hot rodding as we know it was born in Southern California and developed during the 1930s, largely because of the Depression. Young men of driving age who suddenly had no hope of buying a sporty new car (as they had done in the Roaring Twenties) found that they could buy used Model T or A roadsters for next to nothing. Using their own labor and creativity, they could then turn them into fast, exciting cars that would not only attract attention but could beat the most expensive cars on the street from stoplight to stoplight. The cars were built in backyards, and the parts came from junkyards. In most cases fine points such as paint and upholstery

A stripped and channeled '28 Model A roadster, in primer, on the streets of Los Angeles in the early 1940s. The flathead V8 has twin carbs.

From the beginning, the form of the hot rod was determined by its function: to go fast. The first requisite was a hopped-up engine for plenty of power. But to be quick on the street, a car also needs to be light. Fords were the rodders' cars of choice because they were the cheapest and lightest cars made. The roadster body style (a single-seat car with no fixed top or roll-up windows) was universal because it was the cheapest and lightest of all Ford models. Furthermore, with the windshield removed, the roadster had the most streamlined body for dry-lakes racing, where wind resistance is the primary factor limiting high speeds. (Until the late 1940s no closed cars were even allowed to compete at the dry lakes.) These early roadsters also had fenders, bumpers, and other accessories stripped off for the same purpose: weight reduction and streamlining.

Other design elements were initially functional as well. Rods used big tires in the back for traction on the street and high-speed gearing at the lakes. Small tires in the front reduced weight and wind resistance. This tire combination also gave the roadsters a forward tilt known as a "rake."

were last on the list of necessities. These early rodders were very proud of being individuals on the road, driving hot roadsters they had built with their own hands.

Early in the 1930s these roadster jockeys discovered the broad, hard, smooth dry lakes in the high desert northeast of Los Angeles, and they began holding timed speed runs there on summer weekends. Clubs formed with names like Outriders, Low Flyers, Bungholers, Knight Riders, and Sidewinders. The cars were fenderless, hoodless, and topless; they were noisy; and some were painted with flames or other menacing designs. Racing on city streets became a common, dangerous, illegal activity. Early rodding developed not only as a local fad but also as a counterculture. By 1938 this outlaw image had intensified to the point that several of the major clubs organized the Southern California Timing Association to oversee dry-lakes racing, to improve the rodders' public image, and to try to alleviate police harassment; it still is active today.

Rodding grew rapidly after World War II, when builders had more money to spend on their cars, such as this natty red '34 Ford.

This '27 Model T roadster, seen at Bonneville in 1950, has been radically stream-lined. The engine is in the back for rear-wheel traction.

Louvers were punched in hoods to help cool hot engines; they also were added to trunk lids or other areas to release trapped air from car bodies in order to improve their streamlining at high speed. Formed-tube exhaust manifolds and straight, loud pipes increased engine performance. Lowering the chassis or lowering the body over the frame (called "channel-ing") reduced wind resistance and improved cornering capability (a need stimulated by the craze for racing roadsters on oval dirt tracks in the 1940s). In the 1950s, when rodders began running coupes and sedans at the lakes and the new drag races, they chopped the tops low and raked the windshield back strictly for streamlining.

The fact that all these pragmatic modifications also made the hot rods look and sound wicked, mean, and nasty was not lost on the participants. These topless, low, loud, fast, open-wheeled roadsters were exciting to look at and exciting to drive. Even though most of their design elements origi-nated with the desire for speed, rather than any design aesthetic, hot rods

soon adopted specific forms that became traditional and have been repeated for nearly seven decades. Although those forms were initially influenced by racing (whether organized or illegal), hot rods were, from the beginning, made to drive on the street. In fact, the first hot rods were simply an inexpensive alternative form of daily transportation. Today hot rodding is termed a hobby or a sport, but the emphasis is still on driving these vehicles on the street.

Hot rodding and car customizing are based on modifying inexpensive assembly-line vehicles not only to improve their looks and performance but also to personalize them. Creativity is a central element of customizing. The builder is praised for his (and most builders are male) inventiveness and unique touches. No two rods or customs are alike. One of the things that makes hot rodding so much fun is that, unlike in racing or restoration, there are no unbreakable rules. A rodder will be praised by his peers for being daring, for coming up with new tricks, for setting a new trend.

But there is a paradox, for modifications generally are made only within an unspecified but agreed-upon set of parameters. Originally, only roadsters—and preferably Fords—were accepted as rods. Hot rods are lowered in the front, customs are lowered in the back. Hot rods have big tires in the back and little tires in the front, whereas customs have tires (usually whitewalls) that are all the same size, with the rear tires covered by fender skirts. Rodders favor three types of taillights: '39 Ford "teardrops," rectangular '41–'48 Chevy, and round '50 Pontiac. Custom-izers prefer certain wheel covers: the '48–'52 Cadillac "sombrero," the '56 Olds Fiesta, and the '57–'58 Dodge Lancer. A custom never wears small hubcaps. The list of such conventions is endless.

Whether the accepted conventions of rod and custom styling derived from function or aesthetics, the larger issue was the idea of membership, especially in the beginning. The agreed-upon set of parameters for creative modifications, as well as the latest customizing trends or fads, were known solely to the cognoscenti. Cars can be modified or personalized in many ways, but only certain ones are considered true hot rods or customs—members of the cult. Tradition now has as much to do with the accepted styles of rodding and customizing as cultism, but those parameters can still be surprisingly rigid.

Customs were smoothed, rounded, lacquered, and plushly upholstered, like this Barris-built chopped '47 Ford with Cadillac grille and wheel covers.

What began in the 1930s and '40s as hot rodding (though not by that name: the term *hot rod,* of indeterminate origin, did not appear until the mid- to late 1940s) has today multiplied into abundant offshoots, ranging from professional drag racing to dune buggies to bed-dancing mini-trucks. What I call hot rods are technically labeled "street rods" these days, defined by the National Street Rod Association as "modified pre-1949 street-driven vehicles." Today's custom cars are a revival of the 1940s and '50s customs, limited by the Kustom Kemps of America (KKOA) to 1936–64 body styles (though I would select 1960 as a cutoff year to keep the styles more homogeneous). For a period during the 1960s both the traditional hot rod and custom car virtually disappeared from the scene. Here's a brief history.

World War II both put a temporary halt to dry-lake racing (Muroc, the main lake bed, was converted to Edwards Air Force Base) and created the second surge in hot rodding. As Southern California roadster jockeys joined the service and were dispersed to far corners of the world, they described their cars and activities to other servicemen, spreading enthusiasm for rodding. Then, when the war shifted to the South Pacific, thousands of servicemen were processed through bases in Southern California, where they saw and heard these hopped-up roadsters roaring everywhere (mostly in the reckless hands of pre-eighteen-year-old younger brothers). At the war's end the infection spread rapidly across the country. Also significant in the nationwide growth of rodding was the launch in January 1948 of *Hot Rod* magazine, which grew to a circulation of 300,000 in just two years.

As prosperity swelled after the war, rodders were able to spend more money on niceties such as paint, upholstery, and chrome plating. For the first time since the Depression young men could afford to buy new, or nearly new, cars, which many of them took immediately to customizing shops to be chopped, channeled, tuck-and-rolled, and lacquer painted. These late-model customs were cousins to the hot rods, but they were built strictly for style, not speed.

The 1950s was the prime time of hot rodding and customizing. In

1950 the first legal drag strip opened at an airport in Santa Ana, California. At the urging of *Hot Rod* magazine and local police departments, others were soon set up across the country. Thus, organized hot rod racing was no longer limited to the California dry lakes. Custom car shows, often staged by new local car clubs, also sprouted.

In the early 1960s Detroit countered with its own "factory hot rods," the "muscle cars" (such as 409 Chevies, GTO Pontiacs, and 4-4-2 Oldsmobiles), followed by the fast yet affordable Mustang and Camaro "pony cars." By this time most hot rods had either been so hopped up for drag racing or so chromed and cleaned for car shows that they couldn't be driven on the street. Customizing continued to be done on newer cars, primarily for car shows, but the older, outmoded customs were forgotten, and many were junked or crushed. By the late 1960s traditional hot rods and customs had virtually disappeared from the streets.

However, a few small clubs, notably the Los Angeles Roadsters and the Bay Area Roadsters (San Francisco), decided to brazenly drive their show-quality early roadsters on the street, and they organized hot rod get-togethers known as "rod runs." *Rod & Custom* magazine championed this new activity and in 1970 sponsored the first national meet for street rods, in a farmer's field in Peoria, Illinois. Some six hundred cars drove there

A gathering of Los Angeles Roadsters club members (plus one coupe) at Tiny Naylor's drive-in, Hollywood, 1958.

from all over the country, making it by far the largest gathering of hot rods up to that time. Soon new car clubs were being formed and new magazines appeared, focused on pre-1949 modified roadsters, coupes, sedans, and other body styles known as street rods.

As editor of *Street Rodder* magazine in the mid-1970s, I began urging that plentiful and more affordable 1950s cars, mildly customized in the traditional style, be included in this rodding resurgence, and I devoted a couple of issues to the few full-custom, chopped-top '49–'51 Mercuries that existed at that time. Soon custom car clubs were reborn, a national association (the KKOA) was formed, and events for 1950s-style customs, or rods and customs together, began proliferating.

This rebirth of rodding and customizing—propelled largely by members of the now-graying baby-boom generation who built rods in the 1950s, or wished that they had—has continued ever since. At the twenty-fifth annual Street Rod Nationals (held at the sprawling state fairgrounds in Louisville, Kentucky, in 1994) nearly fourteen thousand pre-1949 street rods participated. Little did those Depression-era kids know what they were starting. The following pages capture glimpses of what hot rodding has become today. It's just too bad we can't bring you the action, sounds, and smells that should accompany these pictures. 🛑

A severely lowered '32 Ford roadster with a V-windshield and a
custom-made lift-off steel top.

Hot Rods

*H*ot rods can be mean, they can be cute, they can be simple, or they can be outrageous. Some are wacky, many are colorful, most are loud and fast. There are resto rods, retro rods, techno rods, and race rods, just to name a few. There are highboys, lowboys, fat fenders, and fad cars. But there are some things a hot rod can't be. It can't be subtle. It can't be quiet. Hot rods are not politically correct. And most of all, hot rods should never be taken too seriously. They're strictly for fun.

Technically, a hot rod is any modified vehicle. But if you use the term hot rod almost any place in the world these days, it conjures certain similar images: a yellow, fenderless, chopped-top Deuce coupe like the one in *American Graffiti;* a bright red '33 coupe like ZZ Top's "Eliminator"; a flamed, louvered, and chopped black '34 coupe like "The California Kid" in the Martin Sheen television movie; or, if you're old enough, a wild, flamed T-Bucket roadster like the one Edd "Kookie" Byrnes drove on the TV series *77 Sunset Strip.*

When hot rodding was a fad in the 1930s through the 1950s, the cars were continually updated every time a new trend broke. If the rodders decided, for instance, that wide whitewalls were out and thin whitewalls were in, or that five-spoke mag wheels were the latest thing, your car would be snickered at if it was wearing yesterday's fashion. But now that we're enjoying hot rodding's third-generation splurge, part of the fun is that you can build a car patterned after any of rodding's previous eras. Of course, fresh new trends are continually being established, too, including futuristic rods that rival Detroit's or Tokyo's latest concept cars. But traditional rod styles, especially those of the late 1940s, the 1950s, and the early 1960s, hold up extremely well and are the preference of many current rod builders. Some rodders are even searching out and restoring well-known or classic early hot rods, while others have "cloned" long-lost cars.

And today you don't even need to find a rare '32 Ford or a Model A to build a rod. All of the popular body styles, from T roadsters to chopped '32 sedans to '40 Ford coupes, are available in fiberglass. Several are even available in fresh steel. There are also reproduction frames, custom suspensions, hoods, lights, interiors—you name it—available from today's hot rod companies. All you have to do is buy the combination of parts you want and bolt them together.

Yet there are plenty who feel that real rods must be handcrafted from salvaged original components. A strong contingent is still in it for the original reason: to build fun, exciting, head-turning cars for relatively little cost by using their own labor and ingenuity. More variety, more creativity, more cars, more color, and more fun can be found in hot rodding today than ever, and there are no signs of that changing in the near future. **STOP**

A chopped and channeled
'34 Ford three-window coupe
with a hand-formed track-style
nose and hood.

A chopped and channeled '34 Ford five-window coupe with a big-block Ford Shotgun hemi engine. It has run the quarter mile in 9.30 seconds at 149 mph.

Left: This '36 Willys was named Street Rod of the Year in 1980 by *Hot Rod* magazine. It has dual turbochargers on its small-block Chevy engine.

Right: No two hot rods are alike, but these two red Deuce highboys, built by the same person, come close.

Above left: A scalloped '33 highboy roadster in the traditional style, with polished Halibrand mag wheels and big dirt-track rear tires.

Above right: Under its three-piece hood, this smooth '36 Ford hides a supercharged Chrysler Hemi engine.

Right: This '40 Willys coupe has a supercharged big-block engine and a full roll cage like a race car, but it was built primarily to drive on the street.

Right: This turtle-deck T-Bucket roadster is highly overpowered, with a 6-71 blown Chrysler Hemi with two four-barrels.

Left: The custom fabric top on this fiberglass '32 makes it a "phantom" body style (one never made by Ford).

A pink pearl '32 Chevy roadster, made completely from reproduction steel body components.

A chopped '32 five-window highboy, done in the 1950s style with skinny big 'n' little whitewalls, red wheels, and a flathead engine.

Right: A Deuce highboy with a rolled rear pan, louvered deck, recessed license, Halibrand mags, and a polished quick-change rear end.

Below: Pseudo taxicab styling on a supercharged and fuel-injected Anglia—a small, light car long popular for drag racing.

Remember Kookie's car from *77 Sunset Strip*? This '23 T-Bucket is an exact duplicate, or what rodders call a "clone."

A flamed '40 coupe on a big rake with polished five spokes. Note that the door handles have been removed.

This subtle-looking '34 coupe
has giant tires in the back
because it has a 427 single-
overhead-cam Ford engine
under the hood.

The most effective element
of this low, full-fendered
'32 roadster is its unusual
shade of green paint.

Though numerous copies have
been built, this is the actual
yellow Deuce coupe that starred
in the movie *American Graffiti.*

FICIALLY NOTED

Above: The parachute on this chopped and channeled '34 coupe is primarily for visual effect, but the tunnel-rammed big-block runs ten-second quarter miles.

Right: This '40 Ford coupe has red graphics, steel Rallye wheels, the smooth look, and megaphone pipes.

Right: Recently built from a new steel reproduction body, this '31 Model A roadster on a Deuce frame with a flathead V8 is built to pure late-1940s rod specs.

Left: Cruising Pacific Coast Highway in a flamed '34 Ford sedan.

Right: Rod running in a red '28 roadster, with the top down and the ice chest on the luggage rack. The louvers in the splash aprons are a nice detail.

Left: This chopped '34 highboy coupe has all the right details to make it a perfect hot rod.

Looking both smooth and mean, this chopped '33 three-window coupe has an 800-horsepower, nitrous-oxide-injected small-block to match the image.

Though built recently, this blue
'32 five-window highboy with
red scallops is finished completely in the 1950s style.

A '33 three-window, full-fendered coupe with a chopped top, done in the traditional style with Moon wheel covers.

A full-fendered '32 five-window with a chopped-and-filled top, polished five spokes, and blue scallops.

A chopped, flamed, full-fendered Deuce three-window with polished American five-spoke mags.

We don't see many Model T sedan hot rods. This one, with a supercharged engine and huge grooved rear tires, has a cartoonish quality—which is good.

Regularly street driven, this
supercharged '32, with slicks
and a rollbar added, turns eight-
second quarter miles at nearly
160 mph at the drags.

Opposite: T-Buckets tend to be
the most outlandish of rods, and
this one seems to be all top,
tires, carbs, blower, and pipes.

Arguably the most famous custom is a '51 Merc built for
Bob Hirohata by Barris in 1953 that is undergoing a long
restoration. This is an exact clone.

Cool Customs

Numerous companies—LeBaron, Murphy, Bohman and Schwartz, Brewster—handcrafted custom bodies for automobiles from the outset, but custom cars are something totally different. The customs were born slightly later, and died sooner, than the hot rods—the initial custom-car era being the two decades of the 1940s and '50s. And even though customs are linked closely to hot rods culturally, the two camps have had a not-always-friendly rivalry.

Hot rods were built for speed, but customs were built strictly for style. Although the favored body modifications—chopped tops, extended fenders, rounded corners, filled seams, and so on—all suggest streamlining, this is streamlining for design purposes only. Customs were built for cruising, not racing. The most ardent hot rodders couldn't understand why anyone would spend money on modifications to a car that didn't improve its performance. Many customizers, on the other hand, were content to keep their smoothed and lacquered hoods shut and their drivetrains stock. Further, the lead used to fill and recontour these large, heavy-to-begin-with cars added considerably to their weight, making them that much slower on the street. Rodders derided them as "leadsleds."

Part of the rivalry no doubt stemmed from jealousy. You had to have some bucks to build a custom, since they were made from nearly new cars. The body modifications required considerably more expertise than stripping down a rod and building up its engine, so they were usually farmed out to professional custom shops. The same went for the lush paint jobs and lavish tuck-and-roll interiors. And once this cool custom was completed, you can imagine the impression it made on the young ladies at the soda shop on Friday night. That was part of the plan.

Yet despite being expensive compared to rods, the customs still had that make-it-better, do-it-yourself rebel demeanor. They were built primarily from lower-priced cars such as Fords, Chevies, and Mercuries, but most of the customizing—lowering, lengthening, stretching the front fenders to the rear—gave them the look of more expensive cars like Buicks and Cadillacs. Customizers often incorporated parts from these cars, such as Cadillac grilles and wheel covers, Buick side chrome and fender skirts, and Packard taillights. And while the removal of name badges and other excess chrome cleaned up the lines of the custom, it further disguised the car's identity. Part of the reason for customizing was to lend mystery to the car, to baffle the unknowing, even to make it look sinister.

The rebirth of 1950s-style customizing began in the mid-1970s and, yes, today you can even buy a fiberglass reproduction chopped '51 Mercury. This is largely a nostalgia-driven crowd, and the rivalry between rods and customs is now nonexistent. The smooth shapes, graceful curves, and candy colors of these cool cruisers are a sensual delight. **STOP**

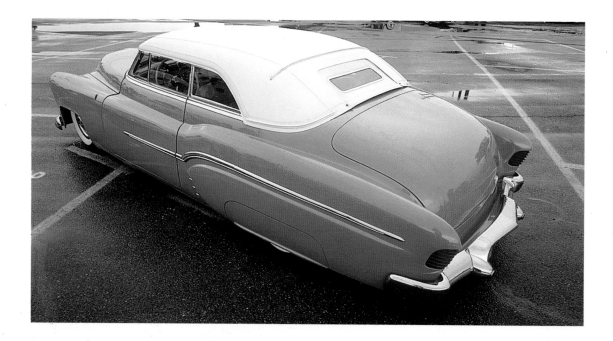

Left: This full-custom '51 Oldsmobile has '54 Merc taillights, gold pearl over persimmon paint, and a chopped Carson-style top replacing the former hardtop.

Right: A 1950s-style chopped '50 Mercury, with '53 Buick side chrome, frenched '54 Buick headlights, a '54 Pontiac grille, and '57 Cad wheel covers.

This mildly customized
'41 Buick fastback with a
lavender Metalflake top sits
extremely low with its hydraulic
suspension retracted.

The drive-in marquee announces *Big* and *The Blob* behind a '58 Buick with a sense of humor, a chopped top, hydraulics, and lavender primer.

A chopped '50 Ford coupe with canted quad headlights, a tube grille, lakes pipes, and pearl blue flames over candy red paint.

Much like the one in *American Graffiti,* this '58 Impala has red tuck-and-roll, Cad taillights, Lancer wheel covers, and gold scallops.

An oxblood '50 Chevy convertible has a lift-off chopped top, frenched lights, a molded '53 Chevy grille with '55 DeSoto teeth, and Packard side trim.

The Dream Truck, a '47 Chevy pickup, was built by several customizers for *Rod & Custom* magazine in the mid-1950s. Wrecked in 1958, it has now been restored.

The Barris brothers chopped a
'40 Mercury, with curved side-
window frames, for Nick
Matranga about 1950. This is
one of the better copies.

The candy yellow paint on this shaved and molded Merc fades from light at the top to dark at the bottom. The grille is from a 1950s Corvette.

At the A&W in a flamed, wire-wheeled '51 Ford.

Right: A chopped, dechromed, wire-wheeled '55 Chevy with a DeSoto grille makes a night pass.

Below: A chopped '50 Merc with bubble skirts, lakes pipes, frenched lights, Moon wheel covers, gold scallops, and a Chrysler Hemi engine.

Right: A cross between a rod and a custom, this fastback '50 Olds 88 has '56 Olds Fiesta wheel covers and green-and-white tuck-and-roll.

Left: Another famous 1950s custom that was wrecked and restored, the X-51 is a sectioned '51 Ford with exaggerated hand-formed fins and taillights.

Left: A late-1950s-style '57 Ford with '58 DeSoto headlights, '55 DeSoto grille, and bullet taillights, finished in candy tangerine paint.

Right: This severely chopped '50 Chevy coupe has a molded '53 grille with extra teeth, filled seams, rounded corners, and chrome reversed rims.

CALIFORNIA
57 HINES

The owner's name is Hines and it's a '57 Chevy. Other touches on this chopped wagon are candy tangerine flames and a '57 Buick grille.

Right: Besides lowering, skirts, lakes pipes, and hood scoops, the major modification to this '49 Buick fastback is the deep candy red paint.

Above: This mild, unchopped, lavender pearl '51 Chevy fastback has flared wheel wells, lots of Corvette teeth, white tuck-and-roll, and Lancers.

Right: This recently restored, candy purple '50 Mercury was chopped and customized for Wally Welch by Gil Ayala of East Los Angeles in 1951. The grille is '51 DeSoto.

Left: This mild '50 Ford sedan has a Pontiac grille, Cad wheel covers, frenched lights, shaved everything, and dazzling candy apple red paint.

Below: A custom-cum-rod, this flamed '50 Ford with a molded '56 Chrysler grille, Moon wheel covers, and big rear slicks has a 6-71 blown Chevy V8.

This mild cream-and-coral '54
Chevy hardtop is nosed, decked,
and shaved, with frenched lights
and ten extra teeth in the grille.

Right: This perfect-stance '51 Ford combines hot rod and custom elements, including frenched lights, whitewalls, Cadillac wheel covers, and a '54 Pontiac grille.

Left: This mild '55 Chevy hardtop has '56 Packard taillights, a molded grille with Corvette teeth, a frenched antenna, and Lancer wheel covers.

Right: A very low, lengthened, and chopped '56 Lincoln with Buick side trim sits in the glow of silly neon chassis lighting.

Below: Another Matranga-inspired '40 Merc hardtop coupe, this purple version has frenched headlights, lakes pipes, and '53 Cad wheel covers.

Customs can be contemporary,
such as this '60 Chevy convertible with a painted tube grille,
hydraulics, and seventeen-inch
billet wheels.

The Barrises chopped and customized this '51 Chevy hardtop for Monsignor Larry Ernst when it was brand new. The restoration is exact.

Left: This classic chopped '49 Merc with a full fadeaway fender line was based on Louie Bettancourt's Ayala-built original.

Below: This '50 Ford coupe goes the full custom route, with a chopped top, recessed cruiser skirts, handmade wheel covers, and tuck-and-roll wheel wells.

Another resurrected early custom (built in Philadelphia in 1953), this chopped '39 Ford convertible blends a '40 Buick grille and a filled hood.

A severely chopped top is the
one major modification to this
'56 Mercury; it doesn't need
any more.

A chopped '36 Cabriolet done
in the 1940s style with a LaSalle
grille, dropped headlights,
DeSoto bumpers, and Buick
teardrop skirts.

A 6-71 GMC blower with two Holley four-barrels on a small-block Chevy plumbed with stainless-steel tubing and braided lines.

Carbs, Blowers, Mills, and Pipes

Although it may sound like a cliché, the engine—or "mill"—is the heart of the hot rod. Even more accurate would be to call it the lungs, because breathing air is more akin to what it does, but we're not going to get too technical here. One description of a hot rod is the biggest engine stuffed into the smallest, lightest car possible. Some rods, such as the T-Bucket roadster, appear to be little more than an engine, a seat, and four wheels. When you drive one of these monsters, you'd better hang on.

In the early days every rodder modified his engine (initially a Model A, B, or C four-cylinder, later the standard-issue Ford flathead V8) as much as he possibly could. But many of the internal engine modifications that made the hottest rods record-setters were the most difficult and the most costly to perform. Besides, just bolting a couple of carburetors, some high-compression heads, and a set of dual exhausts onto one of these under-nourished engines could easily double its power. Therefore, many of the early rodders settled for making their street-driven flathead V8s look and sound pretty much like the fully modified ones, or they added lots of chromed accessories to them (causing hard-core mechanics to sneer, "If it don't go, chrome it"). But if their cars ran reasonably fast on the street, and their engines did not blow apart from being overstressed by all-out racing modifications, they were content.

Most of today's street rod fraternity feels the same way, and the ubiquitous Chevy 350 small-block V8 provides plenty of power for these light cars. But no hot rodder can run an unmodified engine. Internally, it must at least have a big camshaft to give it that rumpity-rump lope at idle. It will invariably have custom tube headers and a throaty exhaust. And even if the owner is content with a single four-barrel carburetor, it must have a custom air cleaner, and the rest of the engine must be covered with chrome or milled aluminum.

Another school of thought holds, "If some is good, more is better." That line of thinking may focus more on making a visual, aural, and kinetic statement than on going as fast as possible, but that's okay. The more carbs the better. How about fuel injection? A blower not only adds lots of power and visual impact but also emits a spur-gear whine that is almost spine-chilling. And today just the use of a well-detailed non-Chevy engine—a nailhead Buick, a Chrysler Hemi, or a nostalgic flathead V8—can bring admiring oohs and aahs from onlookers.

And pipes. All rods and customs have to have pipes. Whether it's just a pair of chromed exhaust tips poking out below (or through) the back bumper, or Funny Car–style zoomie headers sprouting from the engine, the pipes are as important to a rod's look as to its sound. They're part of what makes a hot rod hot. **STOP**

Left: Two Chandler-Grove two-barrels on a Cragar overhead conversion on a Model B four-banger.

Below: A Ferrari V12 with chromed headers and six side-draft Weber carbs in a '32 roadster.

A Cleveland Ford with dual
Holley carburetors on a polished
tunnel ram intake manifold,
reflected in a chromed firewall.

Opposite: A gaggle of T-Buckets with exposed engines, one being a turbocharged Pinto overhead-cam four.

Right: A polished ram induction intake with dual four-barrel carbs on a big-block Chrysler wedge in a T-Bucket.

Left: Blueing on a chromed exhaust header with lakes cap, beside the Pitman arm, drag link, and hairpin radius rod on a highboy.

Dual megaphone pipes straddle
a Jaguar independent rear end
with a mock quick-change
cover and polished Corvette
disc-brake calipers.

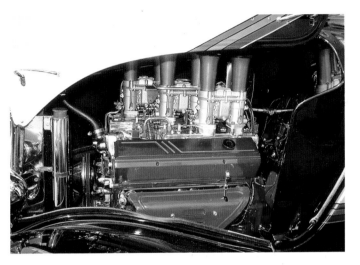

Below: Red-anodized aluminum components, including milled valve covers and bead-rolled, louvered header shields, on a triple-Weber-carbed Chevy.

Above: Ceramic-coated zoomie headers on a 6-71 blown small-block Chevy with two four-barrel carbs.

Right: A Keith Black aluminum Hemi with dual plugs, dual mags, a 10-71 blower, and no fewer than three AFB four-barrel carbs in a Deuce street roadster.

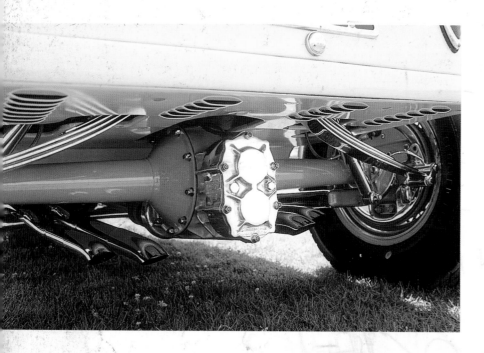

Above: Four chromed pipes under a Model A with a louvered belly pan and a Halibrand V8 quick-change on a chromed buggy spring.

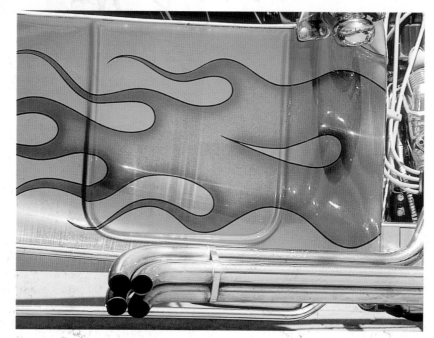

Flames and pipes on a T-Bucket.

Above: Chromed sprint-car-style headers on a nostalgic Deuce, with a woodpecker decal (the "Mr. Horsepower" emblem of Clay Smith racing cams).

A blown big-block Chevy with a simulated bug-catcher injector, Moon breathers, and custom finned aluminum detailing.

Left: Hilborn fuel-injector stacks sprout from a small-block Chevy in a Model A roadster with a front-mounted Moon fuel tank.

Opposite, top left: A Buick nailhead V8 with six two-barrels on a log manifold and plenty of chrome.

Opposite, top right: A small-block Chevy with megaphone headers, three carbs, and a beehive oil filter in a V windshield roadster with painted Mooneyes.

Opposite, bottom left: A neatly detailed big-block Chevy with "no name" (Moon) finned aluminum valve covers and four down-draft Weber carbs.

Opposite, bottom right: Graphics painted on the valve cover of a big-block Chevy with dual quads and nitrous oxide injection.

Dual SuperTrapp mufflers squeeze between the wide rear tires, and under the chromed coil-over shocks, of this Model A roadster.

Pipe, paint, and louvers.

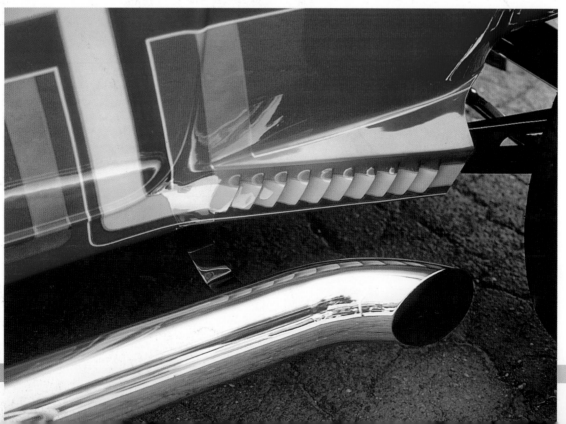

Red plastic fuel lines feeding six pots on a small-block Chevy in a well-used yellow Deuce coupe.

Individual-port electronic fuel-injection on a polished Moon cross-flow Weber intake manifold on a small-block Chevy.

Twin Holley Dominators plus nitrous oxide injection on a Chevy Ratmotor plumbed with braided hoses and formed stainless hard line tubing.

A nailhead Buick with six chromed 97s, finned aluminum valve covers, a finned aluminum valley cover below the carbs, and even a milled-aluminum dipstick handle.

Gold-plated and engraved intake stacks on Weber carbs on a small-block Chevy with engraved 327 valve covers.

Left: Blower-scoop view of a supercharged small-block Chevy with dual four-barrels in a flamed '40 Willys.

Right: A well-blued megaphone exhaust header poking through the louvered and flamed hood of a '32 highboy with chromed and drilled radius rods.

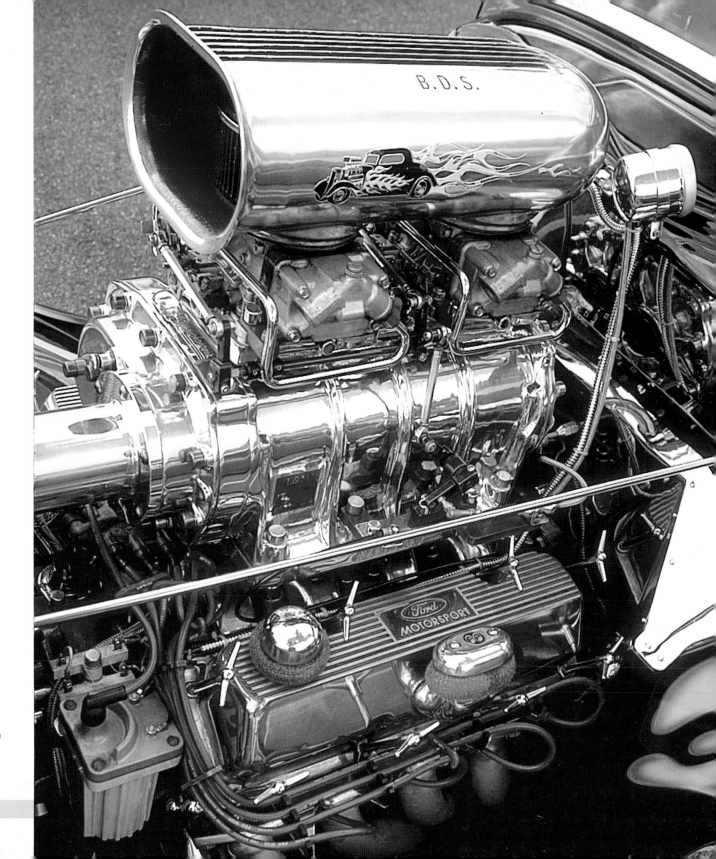

A 6-71 blown Cleveland Ford with twin Holleys in a flamed '34 coupe, wearing tennis wristbands on the breathers to absorb oil blow-by.

Taillight and tailpipe at the back of a '33 Willys.

Triple lakes plugs poke through a molded running board.

Left: A fabricated manifold and air cleaner for a single four-barrel on a 6-71 blower mounted on a GMC inline six in a Chevy sedan.

Right: A now-rare Magnuson dual supercharger with dual side-draft Mikunis on a small-block Chevy with ball mill detailing.

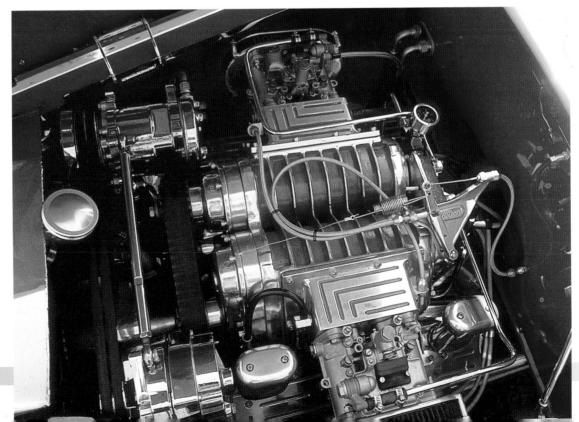

There are several types of American five-spoke mags. This is a rare polished T-70, cut and narrowed for a tiny 145-15 tire on a flamed '33.

Wheels

The wheels are so important to a hot rod that simply installing a set of custom wheels—even just switching the hubcaps—along with lowering the chassis and adding a set of pipes, can be enough to place a car in the rod or custom category. In 1950s slang, someone might refer to his car as his "wheels," or he might tell someone else to "check out that set of wheels." Also, the right wheel-and-tire combination contributes to another element so critical to a hot rod: its stance.

Until the introduction of the mag wheel (so called because the first were made of super lightweight magnesium) in the 1960s, there weren't really any custom wheels. Some dry-lake racers fastened washing-machine lids to their wheels for streamlining (followed later by the spun-aluminum Moon wheel covers manufactured by Dean Moon). Early rodders updated their cars with solid (as opposed to spoke) Ford wheels with small hubcaps. But the custom guys liked full wheel covers, especially the flashy, single-bar "flippers" or "spinners." In the 1950s certain factory wheel covers were in, and customizers would combine parts of wheel covers, adding anything from faucet handles to drawer pulls. Rodders were starting to widen steel wheels or to reverse the rim on the hub, for a race car look. Soon the chrome reversed wheel was all the rage, followed by mag wheels

and ultimately by a torrent of aftermarket cast-aluminum wheels, which are now so common (even on factory cars) that they hold little interest for rodders or customizers.

The latest trend for rods is the "billet" wheel, which has a formed-aluminum rim mated to a center carved from a solid chunk of aluminum by a computer-controlled mill. Another trend is the superwide rear wheel and tire, similar to those on drag cars, known as the "Pro Street look." Both trends now seem to be waning in popularity because of overuse. As the glutted custom wheel aftermarket continues to search for new styles, rodders and especially customizers are finding that some of the older, more traditional wheel-and-tire combinations still work the best.

Whether it's big 'n' little blackwalls on mag wheels, skinny whitewalls with 'caps 'n' rings, high-class chrome wires, Bonneville-flavored Moon wheel covers, or Cad sombreros on a classic chopped Merc, the better rod and custom builders keep coming up with just-right wheel combinations for their cars. Some even keep a second or third set of wheels and tires—for instance, 1940s-era whitewalls and hubcaps to swap with 1960s-era blackwalls and mags—so they can instantly change the car's look, just by changing the wheels and tires. That's how important wheels are to a hot rod. **STOP**

Purple-primered and yellow-scalloped Chevy reflected in a baby Moon hubcap on an after-market chrome reversed wheel.

The billet wheel doesn't match the era, but the Gee Bee racing airplane-style scallops on the red '36 Ford fender around it are great.

The classic Cad sombrero and medium whitewall on a '50 Merc.

Extra-wide polished billet wheel and Pro Street tire on a tubbed '56 Chevy.

Top: Aftermarket Lancer with a checkerboard center painstakingly hand-painted to match the pink on a '55 DeSoto.

Bottom: F-100 'cap 'n' ring on a widened steel wheel on a '40 Ford pickup with some sneaky louvers.

A custom-made wheel cover for a custom car. Note the all-important band of red-painted wheel between it and the whitewall.

Polished Z28 Camaro wheel with fake knockoff and low-profile blackwall on a flamed '47 Ford.

Opposite, top left: The fact that the fenderline is concentric with the tire is all-important on a highboy. The whitewall, yellow wheel, and 'cap 'n' ring help too.

Opposite, top right: Single-bar flippers, or "Hollywood spinners," were the standard on customs in the 1940s. Today's repros aren't as good as the originals.

Opposite, bottom left: Deep, cheap slot mag with a brushed finish and custom-machined hubcap on the back of a smooth Deuce highboy.

Opposite, bottom right: Deep-dish Halibrand—or Halibrand copy—on a candy purple Deuce.

Right: Billet wheel and blackwall on a '34 with megaphone pipes.

Below: A semidirectional five-spoke billet surrounded by hot graphics over candy blue.

Left: Olds Fiesta flipper and medium whitewall on a custom '47 Ford with a '46 Olds grille and a '49 Plymouth bumper.

Right: Polished "directional" billet wheel and blackwall on an aqua '40 Ford.

A highly polished Halibrand and glossy big blackwall on a red Ford woodie.

Lightweight, spindle-mount, magnesium twelve-spoke Halibrands were made for drag cars, but this rodder has adapted disc brakes for street use.

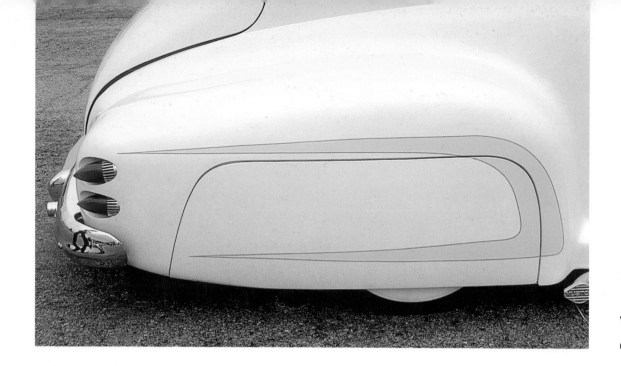

You don't need any wheel covers on the back of a custom.

Torque Thrust D American with a big three-bar knockoff on a deep blue '37 Chevy woodie.

A color-accented Convo Pro with a billet center-nut on a very colorful Pro Street car.

A Boyds billet and blackwall on a cool-flamed '37 Chevy.

Above left: The E.T. III—a two-piece, magnesium, sixteen-inch-diameter rear wheel made for dragsters in the mid-1960s—is considered the ultimate by many rodders.

Above right: Chrome wire wheels were the rage on 1970s resto rods. On the right type of car, they can still look classy today.

Right: This polished five-spoke is surrounded by lush candy red paint on a streamline-style 1940s Studebaker pickup.

A blacked-out Skylark wire on a black '55 Buick, with matching ball mill detailing in the knock-off and portholes.

A '54 Chevy with a wide whitewall, red wheel, single-bar flipper, and some fine red striping.

Chrome reversed wheel, accent-painted center, "Spider" bullet cap, medium whitewall, lakes pipe, and wild flames give good 1960s flavor to a '56 Chevy.

Unpolished five-spoke and 1960s M&H slick with pie-crust sidewall on a vintage Willys Gasser.

Flames in the night on a '50 Merc.

Scallops, Flames, Candies, and Pearls

*I*n the beginning most hot rods were black or some other dark (sinister?) color that looks black in early photos. Of course, in those days lots of roadsters never got as far as shiny paint and were left wearing a suede coat of black primer. Today some rods and customs are intentionally painted black, red oxide, or tinted pastel primer as a throwback fashion statement, while others are coated in jet black, hand-rubbed lacquer to show off flawless metalwork. However, the paint work on most rods and customs now rivals the spectrum, not only in its range of colors but also in its media, textures, varieties of luminescence, and design patterns.

The custom cars of the late 1940s and early 1950s, especially those from the Barris shop in Los Angeles, were the first to be covered in deep, rich, "organic," metallic lacquers, occasionally offset by a light pastel in a two-tone combination. These glasslike paint jobs were sometimes applied in as many as thirty coats. Early in the 1950s, while mixing custom colors at his shop in Oakland, California, Joe Bailon invented what he named "candy apple red" by adding a few drops of translucent red toner to clear lacquer. This produced a rich transparent red that, when painted over a silver or gold base coat, yielded a deep, liquid color that amazed spectators and caught on quickly with customizers. "Candies" come in an array of colors these days and result in a wide range of effects when sprayed over different base coats. One version, sprayed over a glittery base and called Metalflake, was briefly popular during the 1960s but has fortunately fallen out of favor.

Next came "pearls," or pearlescent paints. Originally made by adding finely ground fish scales to lacquer, they create a shimmering effect, like the inside of an abalone shell. The range of other custom paints today is amazing, and what custom painters do with them is even more so.

In the 1950s a small, enigmatic kid from Compton, California, who called himself Von Dutch began using a pinstriping brush and sign paint to make strange, intricate designs on rods and customs. His style, and his antics, have been imitated by hot rod pinstripers ever since. In addition to his distinctive flying eyeballs and other weird creatures, Von Dutch sometimes painted flames or scallops on the hoods of cars—designs that hark back to '30s race cars and even World War I airplanes. Such paint designs, known as "graphics," now range from traditional flames and scallops to splashes, lightning bolts, heartbeat blips, pixels—you name it—sometimes created by designers and generated on computers. In the past, custom paint schemes included everything from fades, fogs, panels, lace, smoke, cobwebs, splatters, fish scales, and ribbons to names, gold-leaf lettering, cartoon characters, and the dreaded airbrush mural. Nevertheless, many know that all a hot rod needs is a smooth, shiny coat of bright red, yellow, or orange to make a visual statement that is plenty strong. ⬟STOP

Candy magenta flames with blue pinstripe outline over yellow on a '34 highboy roadster.

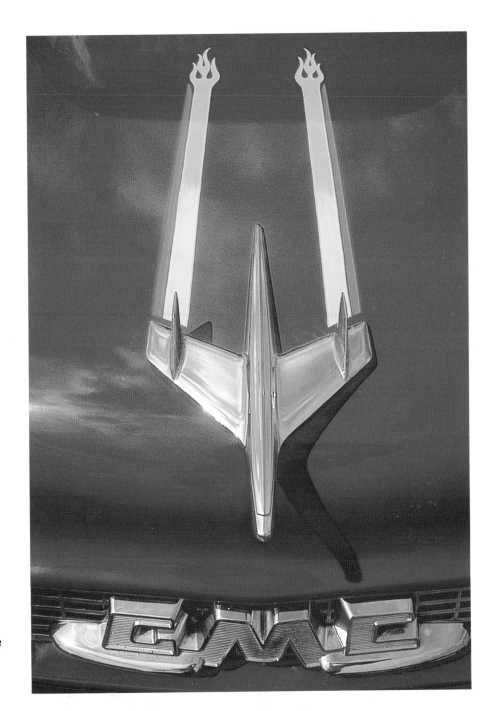

A couple of pinstriped vapor trails with licks off the wingtips of a GMC pickup's hood ornament.

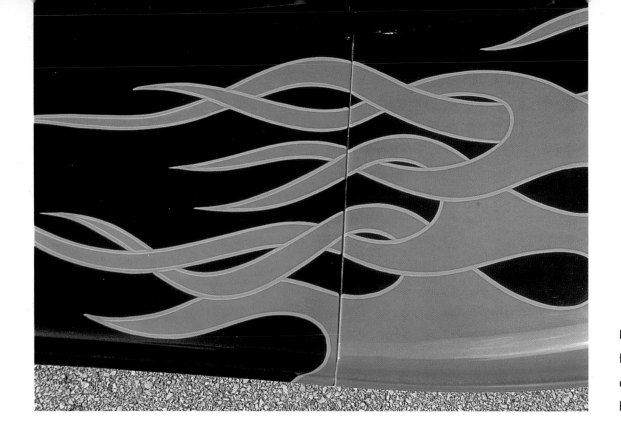

Intertwined purple-and-blue flames over candy wild cherry on the fender and running board of a '32 Ford.

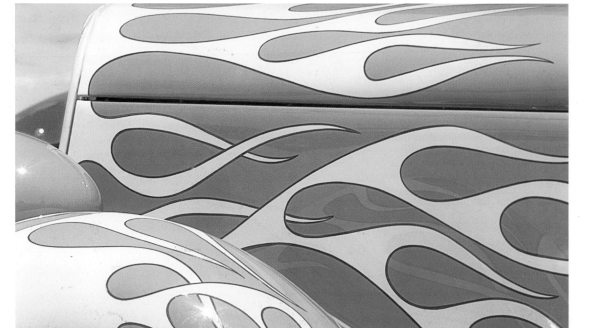

Pink flames over lavender on a '35 Ford. The owner chose the colors from her cosmetics—eye shadow, I believe.

Traditional flames and stripes on a '54 Ford. Look twice—that lower chrome strip is airbrushed art, not metal.

Contemporary candy purple scallops with red-and-blue outlining cover the side and smooth running board on this aqua '40 Ford.

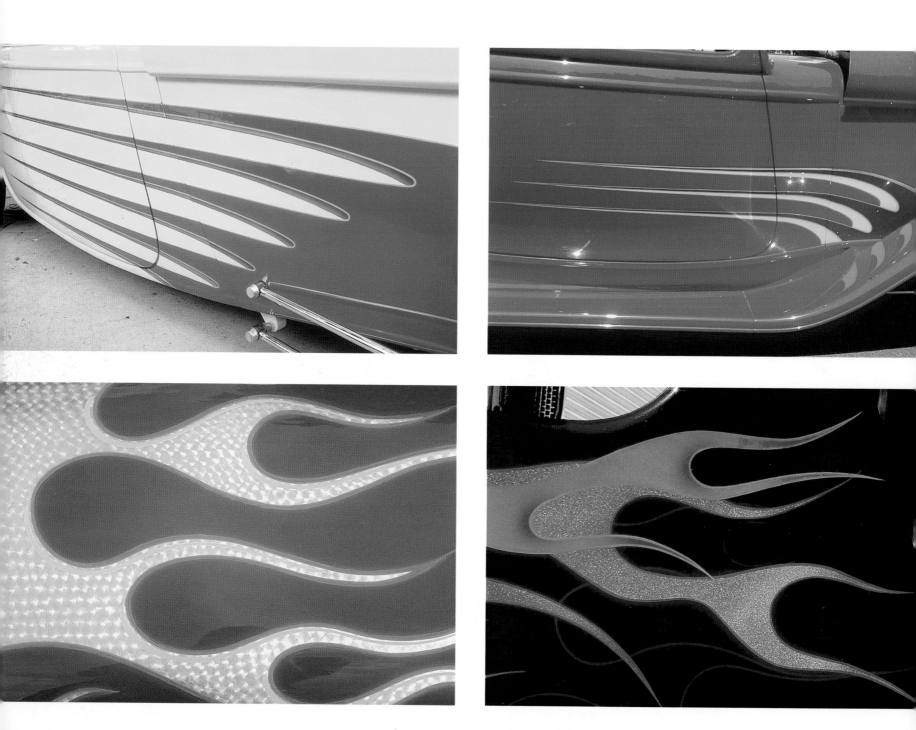

Double Deuce roadsters,
one with exuberant flames
and one with prim pinstripes
and scallops.

Opposite, top left:
Contemporary magenta scallops
with drop shadows on a yellow
channeled '33 roadster.

Opposite, top right: Simple
purple scallops with yellow
drop shadows on a red '32
three-window.

Opposite, bottom left: Engine-
turned, or scrolled, gold-leaf
flames with orange-and-yellow
pinstriping over green.

Opposite, bottom right:
Flame detail with lavender
candy over a Micro-Sequin base,
similar to Metalflake.

Scallops, Flames, Candies, and Pearls • 103

An orange graphic on an aqua-and-purple '37 Ford sedan.

A candy red flame with powder
blue pinstriping over luscious
purple pearl on a '33 roadster.

Popsicle shades of candy colors blended in the flames on the front of a '40 Standard Ford sedan.

Opposite, top left: Pinstripe flames usually look wimpy, but they become a tour de force on this yellow-and-green '55 Buick mild custom.

Opposite, top right: Wild, asymmetrical yellow, orange, and red flames sprout from the toothy grille of a '53 Chevy.

Opposite, bottom left: Wispy purple pearl flames trail down the side of a lime green '54 Chevy.

Opposite, bottom right: White-to-blue candy-blended scallops turn to red lightning bolts on this '34 Ford.

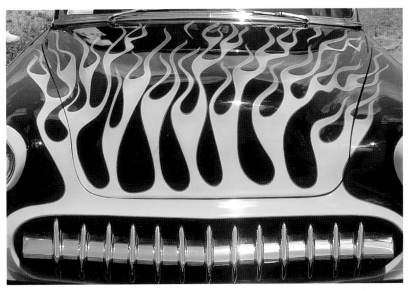

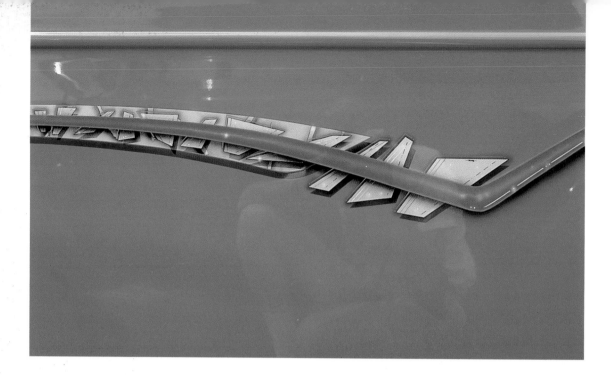

Right: Hot-pink-and-gray beltline graphic over aqua. This was painted with an airbrush, striping brushes, and possibly ink pens.

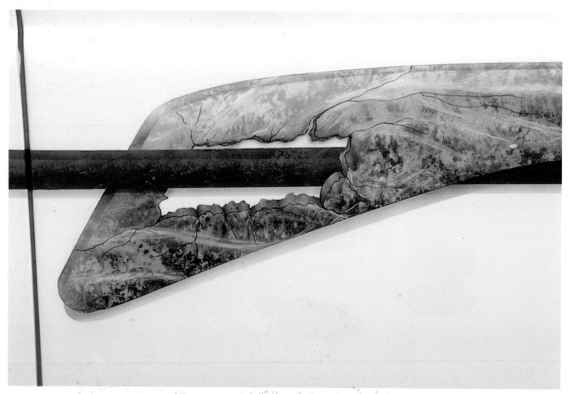

Left: A green marble graphic over white, probably created with a sponge, feather tip, ink pen, and airbrush.

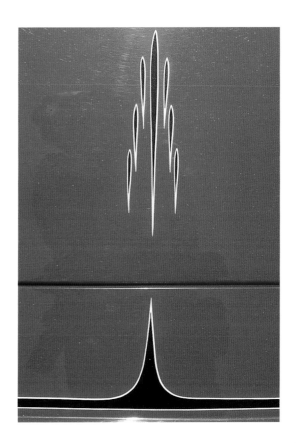

Black-and-white teardrops and scallop on the deck of a '34 coupe in a style popularized by well-known pinstriper Tommy the Greek.

A red '34 Chevy pickup with white scallops and small purple drop shadows.

Left: A traditional pinstripe design on the nose of a '33 Ford, in the style created in the early 1950s by Von Dutch.

Below: Traditional but copious flames by one of the 1960s masters, Dean Jeffries, on his own current rod—a chopped and sectioned '34 sedan.

Opposite, left: This is candy tangerine, at its best.

Opposite, right: Simple, semi-traditional, very effective red scallops with white stripe outlining on a Deuce highboy roadster.

Scallops, Flames, Candies, and Pearls •

Right: Traditional yellow-and-orange flames on the nose of a 1950s-style '40 Mercury.

Below: Pearl magenta flames with orange pinstripe outlines on candy red.

Frenetic purple pearl flames
with silver outlines on a lime
green British '32 Ford sedan.

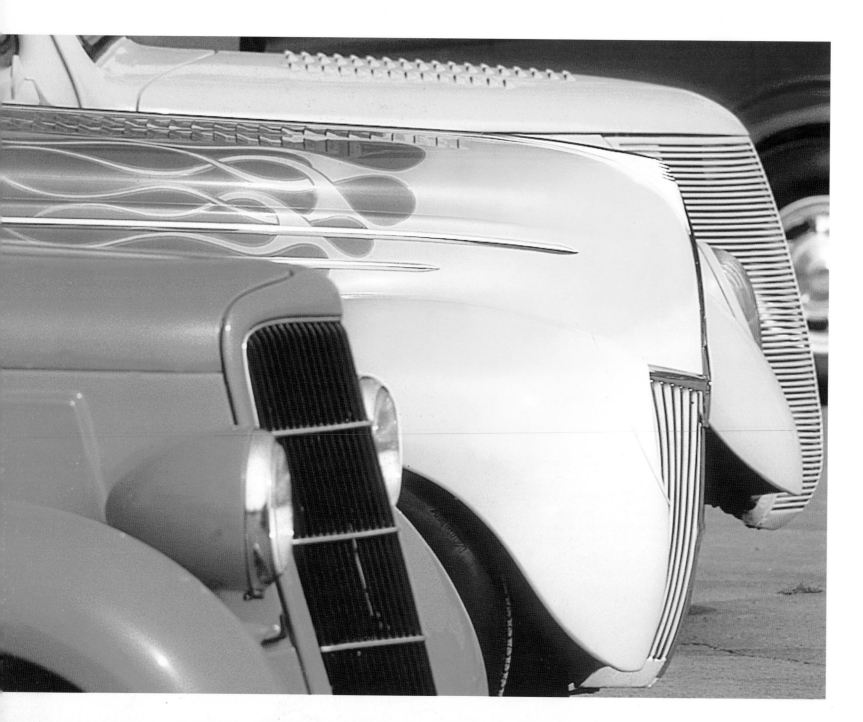

Opposite: Yellow flames over medium blue on a louvered '39 nose between apple green and lemon.

Above: The hood of this '50 Ford seems to glow with white-blended-to-red flames with blue tips and outlines. A simple pinstripe adorns the nose.

A '56 Dodge taillight with '59 Cadillac lenses.

Details, Details

Many hot rods and customs hit you right between the eyes with a visual assault of wheels, pipes, and colors. Subtlety is not one of the characteristics of a rod or a custom. Some rods are much more outspoken than others, yet even on the killer machines, it is often the little things that set one car apart from the crowd. We rodders call it "detailing," and it can work in several ways.

First, consider the car's physical construction. Neatness is a virtue in rod building, and that doesn't apply only to a smooth, flawless paint job. It means that the door jambs, the engine compartment, and the underside of the hood and trunk are all sanded, painted, rubbed, and waxed, just like the exterior of the body. It means that the gaps between the doors, hood panels, trunk, and body are all the same width. It means that all the wiring in the car is neatly routed and tie-wrapped in bundles of perfectly parallel wires. The same goes for fuel and brake lines. Even though they're driven on the street, many of today's rods are painted, plated, polished, and otherwise detailed from the frame up.

Another aspect of detailing concerns the selection or construction of component parts. It may be a matter of choosing exactly the right combination of traditional rod or custom components and installing them a certain way. For instance, one outspoken traditional rod builder asserts that '32 five-window coupes should have '39 Ford taillights, that three-window coupes should have '47 Chevy taillights, and that roadsters need '50 Pontiac taillights—and that they can't be too far apart or too close together. Another enhancing detail might be the use of a component that no one else has tried and that suits the car perfectly. Or it might be constructing or machining custom engine-accessory brackets, or simply chroming, polishing, or drilling "lightening" holes in existing ones.

Finally, it's the small, creative details—the unique custom touches that an individual adds to his car—that really get the attention and admiration of fellow rodders and customizers. It might be a 1950s antenna recessed into the flank of a custom Buick or a pair of carved maple door handles on a woodie wagon, but it makes the seasoned rod fancier do a double take. Or it could be an inventive combination of such elements that adds up to an overwhelming car.

You might not spot all the point-scoring tricks in the following photos unless you're a veteran rodder, but by now you should be getting a pretty good idea of what makes rods hot and customs cool. **STOP**

Streamline moderne door handle and chrome strip on a '40 coupe, with gold-leaf flames and a Lady Luck decal.

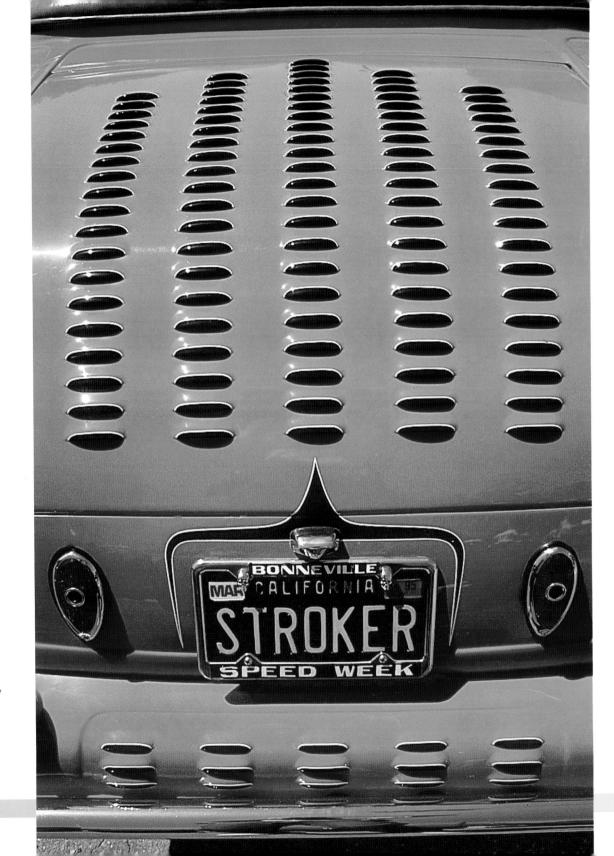

Louvers in a '32 roadster
deck and gas tank (welded on),
black-and-white pinstripes,
'39 taillights with blue dots,
and a black-painted license.

Right: Ford accessory side mirror on a '41 Mercury Woodie.

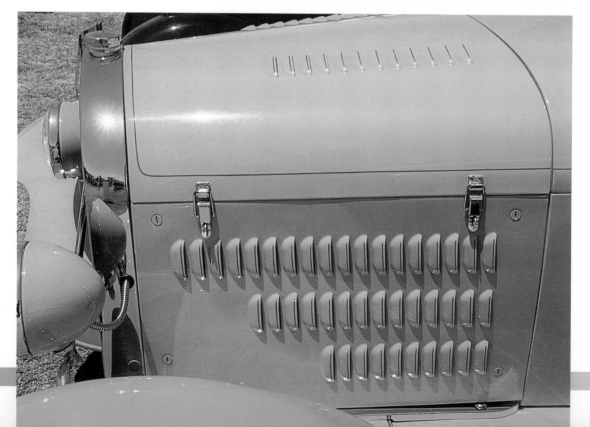

Left: Louvers, pinstripes, and tool-box latches on a three-piece '29 Model A hood.

Left: Frenched '41 Studebaker taillight, recessed Corvette bumper, molded pencil-tip exhaust, and rounded trunk corner on a pearl lavender '41 Ford.

Right: Recessed '59 Cad taillights on a candy blue '50 Merc in the rain.

Opposite, top left: Dual sunken antennas.

Opposite, top right: Carved wooden door handles on a Ford woodie.

Opposite, bottom left: Flush-fit hand-formed fender skirt on a '53 Buick.

Opposite, bottom right: Re-formed side scoop on a '60 Chevy.

Greyhound radiator cap on a '34 roadster, surrounded by severely weather-checked candy tangerine paint (not good).

Below: Mooneyes on a Model A roadster on Deuce rails with semi-hairpin radius rods.

Left: Painted Deitz headlight with teardrop pinstripes, finned aluminum Buick brake drum, and chrome with orange paint accents on a yellow Model A.

Asymmetrical megaphone
pipes, club plaque, chromed
rear-end housing and shocks,
louvered pan, and '39 teardrops on a Model A.

Above: Stewart-Warner gauges, Rat Fink decal, eight-ball shift knob, drilled race car steering wheel, connecting-rod column support, and white tuck-and-roll.

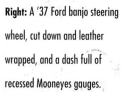

Right: A '37 Ford banjo steering wheel, cut down and leather wrapped, and a dash full of recessed Mooneyes gauges.

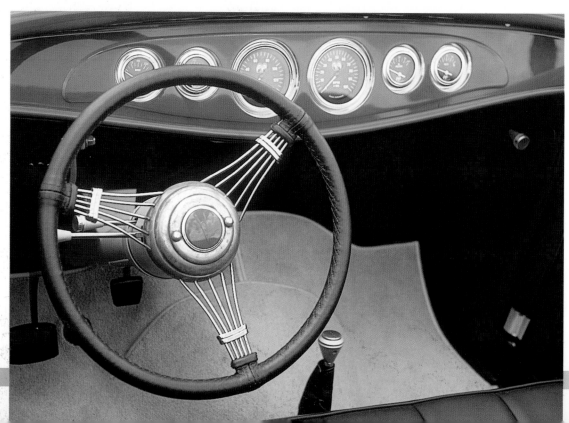

Right: A flying eyeball painted on a filled '32 grille shell, imitating Von Dutch's personal emblem.

Below: Patterned after the logo for Clay Smith Cams, this stylized woodpecker with flaming hair is hand-painted on the frame rail of a green '32 highboy roadster.

Opposite: Original '32 Ford
sedan door handle, accented
by stripes.

Filigree blue pinstripe design by
Butchr, at the back of a deep
purple pearl hot rod.

Above: A '39 Ford teardrop taillight with a red-over-gold pinstripe accent on a red '32 roadster.

Right: A 1950s swept-back aerial recessed into the rear quarter of a peach '47 Buick convertible custom.

Left: Twin antennas, mounted in '56 Buick chrome portholes, in the rear fender of a powder blue '50 Ford.

Above: A '40 Ford chevron taillight with tiny teardrops top and bottom.

Left: A '37 Ford V8 emblem trunk handle offset by a pair of simple white pinstripes.

Crazy eyeballs painted inside the pop-up cowl vent of a '38 Standard Ford with a louvered hood and dechromed grille.

Original winged emblem and

chief's-head cap on a lavender

'34 Pontiac.

Leather hood strap, racing
number, Gilmore oil emblem, and
T lights on a cut-down A bar on a
track-style '27 Model T roadster
with a suicide front end.

Left: A shaved '50 Merc bumper with inset bubble taillight and molded-on Kaiser guard incorporating an exhaust tip, against a candy yellow body.

Above: A now-rare '56 Mercury station wagon taillight on a coral-and-white '56 Ford.

Opposite: Louvers, delicate pinstripes, '39 teardrop taillight, and an appropriate slogan at the tail of a red Deuce roadster.

Augmented personal plate in a polished billet frame with third brake light, recessed in the rear pan of a '34 Ford.

Glossary

You can't talk hot rods and custom cars if you don't know the lingo. The following is just a cursory sampling of hot rod jargon. New terms are, of course, being introduced constantly. Terms in SMALL CAPITALS have their own entries.

A-bone A '28–'31 Ford hot rod (Model A); derived from the term "T-bone" for Model T's.

aftermarket Technically, any component, including replacement parts, not made by the original auto manufacturer. But rodders tend to use the term primarily for products made by specialty companies for rods and customs.

baldy; beanie See MOON.

beater A rod or custom that is unfinished (perhaps permanently), probably in primer paint, but driven regularly. Also, a rod or custom that was finished at some point but has since deteriorated from much use.

beauty rings See 'CAPS 'N' RINGS.

big-block A large V8 engine, with a physically larger block, usually of 400–450 cubic inches. A Chevy big-block is also known as a "Rat" or "Ratmotor."

big 'n' littles Big (especially tall) rear tires and small front ones.

billet Used as a noun or adjective to describe parts that have been machined or otherwise cut from a solid piece (or billet) of aluminum; not cast or welded. A "billet wheel" has a billet center attached to a formed-aluminum rim.

billet look A STREET ROD style highly popular in the 1980s, with all chrome and any other protuberances (i.e., hinges, handles) cleaned off the body, billet wheels, and numerous components (dash panel, windshield posts, taillight housings, mirrors, license frames, and possibly the grille) made from brush-finished billet aluminum.

blower Any type of supercharger, but most often a belt-driven ROOTS-STYLE supercharger that sits on a V8 engine with the CARB(S) on top of it.

blown Supercharged; said of an engine. It also describes an engine that has exploded from being over-stressed.

Bondo A common brand of plastic body filler, often used as a generic term. Use of too much Bondo, rather than good metalworking, to make body changes or to fill dented or rusty areas is highly frowned upon.

Bondo barge A car that has been customized or repaired with too much plastic filler.

B pillar See HARDTOP.

bubble skirts See SKIRTS.

buggy spring A single, transverse leaf spring suspending the front or back of the car, as on pre-1949 Fords.

candy, candy apple A transparent paint, tinted in any Kool-Aid color, that is applied over a reflecting base coat—usually gold or silver—to produce a deep, rich hue.

'caps 'n' rings Small hubcaps (usually early Ford) and beauty rings (thin, snap-on, chrome trim bands near the wheel's outer lip) on painted steel wheels.

carb Short for *carburetor*, a fuel system that relies on the suction of a venturi (a narrowing of the inlet throat) to draw a metered amount of fuel into the airstream before it enters the cylinders. Also called a "pot" or "jug."

Carson top A nonfolding, padded, usually CHOPPED, lift off convertible top made by the Carson Top Shop in Los Angeles. Many other upholstery shops made Carson-style tops as well.

channel To lower the car body over the frame, which requires cutting out and raising the floor.

chop To lower the roof by cutting and rewelding; on ROADSTERS, to cut down the windshield.

chrome reversed wheel A chrome-plated steel wheel that has had the center cut out, reversed, and welded back in to make the wheel look wider or "deeper" (because the back side of the rim—now facing front—is wider).

coupe A closed, two-door car with a short roof and one seat. A 1950s coupe might have two seats but always a shorter roof than a SEDAN.

custom A post-1934 vehicle with a body that has been modified for sleekness and smoothness. Customs usually sit very low, generally more so in the rear.

cutouts See LAKES PIPE.

dago See RAKE.

deck To remove any ornaments, emblems, or handles from the trunk, and then weld and fill the holes.

Deuce A 1932 Ford—the first V8 model and arguably the most popular hot rod body style. The name obviously refers to the 2 in the year, but there's a devilish connotation as well.

drag A two-car straight-line acceleration race from a dead stop, initially from stoplight to stoplight on the street but now (preferably) on a quarter-mile "strip." "The drag" or "the main drag" also refers to the primary cruising street in a town, and this might be the derivation of the racing term—"to race the drag." It might also have come from the challenge to race—"drag it out, and let's see what she'll do."

drag link On a solid front axle, the bar that connects the steering box to the spindle, to turn the wheels.

dropped axle A solid (I-beam or tube) front axle with the outer ends raised, which lowers the car.

fad car A name given to T-BUCKETS in the late 1960s, when they were extremely popular; also known as a "Fad T."

fade, fadeaway A paint job that blends one color or shade into another. "Fadeaway" also refers to front fenders

on '39–'48 Ford, Merc, or Chevy customs that have been extended to the rear fenders, giving a streamlined fender line like that on similar vintage Buicks. Also used to describe '49–'51 Mercs with the "hump" taken out of the door.

fat fender A car with round, bulging, removable fenders, front and rear; specifically, '35–'48 Fords and '40–'48 Chevies.

filled Generally refers to any part of a car body that has been welded and then smoothed with filler—for example, where a handle or ornament has been removed or where seams, such as fender to body, have been closed.

five-spoke Any MAG wheel with five spokes in the center, but more specifically such wheels made by the American Racing wheel company in several similar styles.

five-window A COUPE with five windows, not counting the windshield.

flames, flamed A paint scheme of stylized, usually undulating flames that cover the nose, hood, or sides of a car. No rodder or racer would want his engine to be really on fire, but flames imply a truly hot car and give a menacing look.

flathead Any valve-in-block engine, but specifically the '32–'53 Ford and Mercury V8.

flipper A wheel cover with one, three, or four raised bars that reflect light as the wheel turns; also known as a "spinner."

four bar A type of RADIUS ROD set-up using two separate, pivoting parallel bars on each side of the frame.

french To mold the headlight or taillight housings to the body and install the lenses from the backside, often in a

recessed manner. The term derives from the appearance of french cuffs. Also applies to any recessed component (e.g., an antenna) or one with a raised lip around it (e.g., an exhaust pipe).

fuel injection A fuel system that uses a high-pressure pump and either mechanically or electronically metered nozzles to squirt fuel into the airstream entering the cylinders, usually with a separate nozzle for each cylinder.

Funny Car Originally (in the mid-1960s), a DRAG racing class for high-powered stock-body cars that had the front and rear wheels moved forward for better traction and steering, which made them look funny. Now they use tilt-up fiberglass bodies slightly resembling new cars, a tube chassis, and nitromethane-burning supercharged aluminum HEMI engines.

Gasser A 1960s DRAG racing classification for full-bodied, technically street-drivable, often supercharged cars that ran on gasoline. The '33–'41 Willys was a very popular body style in this class.

gennie See STOCK.

gow job Early name for a hot rod, obviously derived from "go job," as opposed to a show job. Also known as a "hop up" or "soup up."

hairpin A type of front-axle RADIUS ROD made from U-shaped bent tubing, resembling a large hairpin.

hardtop A closed car, primarily of the 1950s, with no door post, or "B pillar."

header An exhaust manifold made of individual tubes that have been bent and welded together.

hemi Any engine with hemispherical combustion-chamber heads; when capitalized it refers specifically to the '51–'57 and '64–'71 Chrysler V8 versions. A "Shotgun hemi" is a rare Ford Boss 429, only a few hundred of which were made in 1969–70.

highboy A pre-1935 Ford COUPE, ROADSTER, or SEDAN with the fenders removed and the body sitting on top of the frame (not CHANNELED). For Model T's and A's, a highboy is a body thus mounted on a '32 frame. Highboys can still be very low.

high tech Contemporary rod styling featuring smooth bodies, minimal or painted-out chrome, and brush-finished bare metal (especially BILLET aluminum); the BILLET LOOK.

hop up See GOW JOB.

hot rod A term of unknown origin, probably derived from "hot roadster." In the 1940s it was considered a pejorative, commonly used in newspaper accounts of kids in jalopies racing on the street. Today, it encompasses a wide variety of vehicles modified for improved looks and/or performance (with emphasis on performance), but purists use it to refer only to modified cars from 1948 (or even 1934) and earlier.

Jimmy Short for a GMC BLOWER (see 6-71) or a GMC in-line six-cylinder engine.

jug See CARB.

kemp In the 1950s, a slang (specifically beatnik) term for cars in general. Today it has been appropriated by certain adherents to mean a custom car, or Kustom Kemp (as in the Kustom Kemps of America [KKOA], a national association for 1935–64 customs).

kickstand See LAKES PIPE, LAKERS.

knockoff A threaded center cap with two or three prongs or "bars" that holds a racing wheel onto a hub with a threaded center. At pit stops, tires are quickly changed by hitting the knockoff on one of its bars with a hammer to loosen it, spinning it off, spinning it back on to hold the new wheel, and hammering it tight. MAG or spoke wheels are often decorated with simulated knockoff caps.

kustom In the early 1950s, for some unknown reason, the well-known customizer George Barris always spelled *custom,* as well as other *c*-words, with a *k*. His shop was called Kustom City; he promoted a loosely knit organization called Kustoms of America; and one of his custom trucks was called the Kopper Kart.

lakes pipe, lakers Originally, a HEADER with a cap (also known as a "lakes plug" or "cutout") that could be removed quickly for racing at the dry lakes without removing the mufflers. Today, a long, chromed, decorative pipe, with a cap at the end, that is mounted along the bottom edge of the body on a custom; also called a "kickstand."

leaded, leaded-in Before plastic filler (see BONDO), molten lead was used to fill, smooth, or recontour body areas. Anywhere holes were filled or seams were molded, the body was described as "leaded-in."

leadsled, sled Originally a derogatory term for customs in general (as used primarily by hot rodders), but especially for one on which body modifications were made by paddling on lots of lead rather than reshaping the sheetmetal (or "metalworking").

lowboy A CHANNELED, fenderless car.

lower To drop the body closer to the ground, usually by cutting or flattening the springs or by reworking the suspension.

mag Short for *magnesium,* an extremely light alloy used to make cast racing wheels. A mag wheel, or "mag," now refers to any cast-aluminum AFTERMARKET wheel. Also short for *magneto,* a self-contained, high-voltage ignition distributor. And short for *car magazine,* to which most rodders are addicted.

megaphone Either a HEADER (which exits horizontally from the engine, on either side of the car) or an exhaust pipe tip with a long, conical shape.

Metalflake, flake A kind of paint job consisting of CANDY paint sprayed over tiny aluminum-foil squares, like glitter. It is considered gaudy or gauche today, which it always has been.

mild custom A car that has been customized moderately (NOSED, DECKED, FRENCHED, LOWERED, painted, upholstered, and so on). A "radical custom" is one that has been CHOPPED, CHANNELED, or SECTIONED.

mill An engine; specifically an internal-combustion engine—which most rodders would argue should never be called a "motor."

milled Cut, shaped, or detailed on a milling machine; machined. Said of BILLET aluminum.

Moon A large, convex, spun-aluminum wheel cover to streamline wheels, made by the Moon Equipment Co. A "baby Moon" is a small, rounded, chrome hubcap, also known as a "beanie" or "baldy."

nailhead A '53–'66 Buick V8, so called because its valve covers are vertical and the heads of its valves are small, making them resemble nails.

nerf bar In circle track racing, bumping another car was called "nerfing." Builders attached bars at the nose and tail, and ahead of the rear tires, to protect against nerfing; these came to be called "nerf bars." On a rod, it refers to any small bumper made of tubing, usually chromed.

97 A type of Stromberg two-barrel carburetor common on hot rod engines of the 1940s and '50s.

nosed Having the hood ornament and any chrome emblems removed from the hood, with the holes welded and filled.

pearl, pearlescent Custom paint originally made with ground fish scales (now made from mica particles), which shimmers like the surface of a pearl or an abalone shell. It can be mixed into, or applied over, any color of paint.

phone booth An unchopped '28–'29 Model A pickup or Model T COUPE.

pinstripes Thin lines hand-painted with a special brush ("dagger") on top of the body color, either accenting body lines or creating abstract designs. Von Dutch of Los Angeles created hot rod–style pinstriping in the early 1950s. Tommy the Greek of Oakland, California, had his own distinctive striping style using two-color lines and "teardrops." Also known as "stripes" or "striping."

pipes Exhaust pipes, especially the chrome portion at the rear of the car.

pot See CARB.

Pro Street A type of late-model street car built to look like Pro Stock class DRAG cars with huge, wide rear wheels and tires in TUBBED wheel wells, a full roll-bar cage, and other race car accessories. It also refers to the wheels and tires themselves.

quarter A quarter-mile DRAG strip for standing-start races.

quick-change An AFTERMARKET REAR END with a removable rear cover and an extra set of easily changeable gears for altering the gear ratio.

race rod A STREET ROD with a high-powered engine and safety equipment, allowing it to run at DRAG races, though still remaining street legal.

radical custom See MILD CUSTOM.

radius rod A single or multibar link that pivots on the frame rail and attaches to a solid front axle, on either side of the car, to hold the axle in alignment while allowing it to move up and down on the spring(s).

rake The stance of a car with the front lowered more than the rear. Also known as a "dago," from "dago" DROPPED AXLES, which were made in San Diego by Ed Stewart during the early 1950s.

Ratmotor, Rat See BIG-BLOCK.

rear end The complete rear-axle assembly of a car.

resto rod A style of rod with a restored body and all the original accessories, such as lights, mirrors, handles, and luggage rack, as well as chrome wire wheels in most cases. Popular in the 1970s.

retro rod A current hot rod styled to an earlier era, especially the 1940s or '50s.

roadster An open car (no solid roof) with one seat, a removable windshield, and no roll-up side windows. The cheapest and lightest model in the line, yet sporty.

Roots-style A type of pump or supercharger, invented by the Roots brothers in 1854, that uses two parallel, meshing rotors that spin in opposite directions inside a case, pumping an equal volume of air (or other matter) with each revolution, thus making it a positive displacement blower.

rubber rake The RAKE caused by BIG 'N' LITTLE tires.

scallops A paint design of long, usually thin, tapered spears, either flowing backward from the nose of the car or intertwined throughout the body panels.

section To cut a horizontal portion out of the car's body to make it thinner. Obviously a major operation.

sedan A closed two- or four-door car with a long roof and front and rear seats.

shave To remove any chrome or other protruding parts, such as door handles. A NOSED and DECKED car has been shaved.

6-71 A ROOTS-STYLE supercharger made by GMC and originally used on a two-stroke diesel engine with six cylinders of seventy-one cubic inches each. Such BLOWERS were also made by GMC in other sizes, such as 4-71, and by AFTERMARKET companies in larger sizes, such as 10-71.

skirts Removable metal covers—favored by custom owners—that attach to the rear fenders, hiding the wheel and tire. Certain factory accessory types, such as the '40s Buick "teardrops" and the '57 Mercury "Turnpike Cruisers," were popular, as were hand-made varieties such as the long, bulging "bubble skirts."

slammed Severely LOWERED, especially in front.

sleeper A car that looks unmodified on the outside, or looks like a BEATER, but has a big, high-powered engine hidden under the hood.

slicks Wide, soft, untreaded rear tires that provide maximum traction for DRAG racing.

small-block A medium-size V8 engine, usually 300–350 cubic inches.

sombrero A recent nickname given to the large

'49–'52 Cadillac wheel covers—shaped much like a Mexican hat—that were standard on most early 1950s customs.

soup up See GOW JOB.

spinner See FLIPPER.

spot A bullet-shaped spotlight mounted through the windshield pillar. A "dummy spot" has no inside handle or working light.

stock Unmodified; as built by the factory or original equipment manufacturer (OEM). Also known as "gennie."

street rod Originally, a hot rod built primarily to drive on the street, as opposed to one built for racing. Since the late 1960s–early 1970s, it has been defined as a pre-1949 street-driven hot rod.

stripes See PINSTRIPES.

suicide front end A solid-axle front suspension that places the axle ahead of the BUGGY SPRING for increased lowering, used primarily on T-BUCKETS.

tach Short for *tachometer*, a gauge that reads engine speed in revolutions per minute (RPMs).

T-bone See A-BONE.

T-Bucket A fenderless hot rod using a pre-1926 Model T ROADSTER body (usually fiberglass) and a simple tube frame, with either a severely shortened pickup bed, a turtle deck (trunk), or just an exposed gas tank in the back.

techno rod A HIGH TECH hot rod.

three-window A COUPE with three windows, not counting the windshield. Ford made them from 1932 through 1936.

tubbed A vehicle that has had the rear frame and REAR END narrowed, the wheel wells cut out, and larger wheel-well "tubs" installed to allow superwide PRO STREET rear wheels and tires.

tuck-and-roll A type of upholstery, usually in Naugahyde, with rows of narrow, stuffed pleats in vertical or horizontal patterns (or both), popular in rods and customs.

Tudor In the 1930s and '40s Ford called its two-door SEDAN model a Tudor, and its four-door model a Fordor. Most of the several body styles were also sold in Standard and De Luxe versions, which had completely different grilles from 1937 through 1940.

tunnel ram A tall, open-plenum, long-runner intake manifold, usually for two four-barrel CARBS.

turbo Short for "turbocharger," a type of centrifugal supercharger driven by exhaust gas pressure.

V-windshield As its name implies, a ROADSTER windshield with a swept-back V-shape. One popular type was made by George Du Vall in Los Angeles. Others were custom-built or adapted from speedboats.

wide whites Tall, skinny tires with four- to five-inch-wide whitewalls, used in the 1920s and '30s. Medium whitewalls (often also called "wide whites"), used in the 1950s, have three-inch white bands. Narrow whitewalls, used in the 1960s, have one-inch bands in the middle of the sidewall.

zoomies HEADERS with individual pipes that exit down from the engine, then turn upward, as used on dragsters and FUNNY CARS.

Index